ART
UP CLOSE
From Ancient to Modern

Claire d'Harcourt

chronicle books · san francisco

To Victor, Espérance, and Valentine

Originally published in France in 2000 by Éditions du Seuil/Le Funambule
under the title *L'Art à la loupe: De l'antiquité à nos jours.*

Many thanks to Philippe Sénéchal, scientific adviser for the Institut National d'Histoire de l'Art and lecturer at the University Paris-IV, for his generous and attentive re-reading of the text of this work; the team at Seuil Jeunesse for its efficient help and patience; Béatrice Fontanel, Marion Paoli, and Dominique du Peloux for their judicious advice; and Marie-Geneviève Guesdon, curator of Arabic manuscripts at the Bibliothèque Nationale de France, Keiko Kosugi, curator of Oriental manuscripts at the Bibliothèque Nationale de France, Gisèle Lambert, curator of the print department at the Bibliothèque Nationale de France, and Jean-Christophe Ton-That, in charge of documentary study at the Musée National des Thermes et de l'Hôtel de Cluny, for their valuable knowledge.

Editorial and graphic concept by Claire d'Harcourt.
Design by Double.
Translated by Shoshanna Kirk-Jegousse.
English type design by Susan Greenwood Schroeder.
Typeset in Frutiger and Providence-SansBold.
Manufactured in China.
ISBN-10 0-8118-5464-7
ISBN-13 978-0-8118-5464-1

The Library of Congress has catalogued the previous edition as follows:
D'Harcourt, Claire, 1960-
[L'Art à la loupe. English]
Art Up Close : from ancient to modern / by Claire d'Harcourt.
p. cm.
Summary: Invites the reader to search for tiny details hidden in famous works of art, providing information about each painting, the techniques used to create them, and how the artists and movements helped art to develop through the ages. Answer key features lift-up flaps.
ISBN 2-02-059694-6
1. Art appreciation—Juvenile literature. 2. Picture interpretation—Juvenile literature.
3. Toy and movable books—Specimens.
[1. Art appreciation. 2. Picture puzzles. 3. Toy and movable books.]
I. Title.
N7440 .D4713 2003
709—dc21
2002152175

Distributed in Canada by Raincoast Books
9050 Shaughnessy Street, Vancouver, British Columbia V6P 6E5

10 9 8 7 6 5 4 3 2 1

Chronicle Books LLC
85 Second Street, San Francisco, California 94105

www.chroniclekids.com

When you look at great works of art up close,

you discover that they're teeming with tiny details.

In this book, we've chosen 23 of the

world's greatest **masterpieces**

and enlarged some of their

details. It's your job to locate all

of the **details** in each picture.

In case you have trouble, we've provided **keys**

under the flaps at the end of the book, along with

information about the lives of the artists. To learn more

about each type of artwork, turn to page 50. The stories

there make up a short and fascinating **history of art**

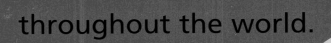

throughout the world.

Egyptian papyrus From The Book of the

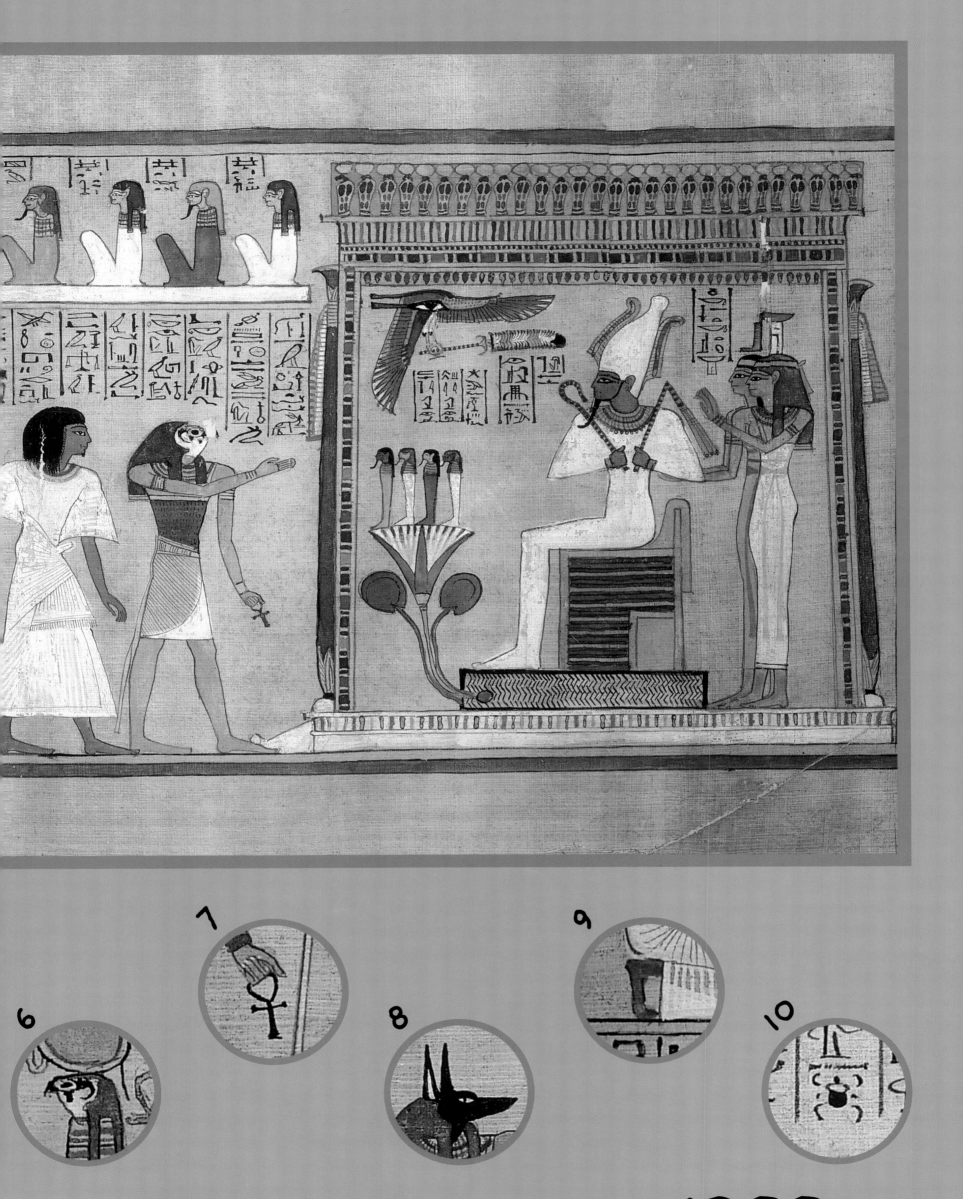

6 7 8 9 10

Dead by the royal scribe Hu-Nefer circa 1300 B.C.

1

2

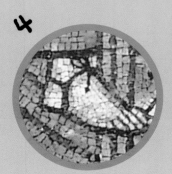

3

4

5

6

Byzantine mosaic

The Sacrifice of Isaac 6th century A.D.

7

Arabic manuscript The Book of

Nativities by Abu Ma'shar 15ᵗʰ century A.D.

9

1

2

3

4

5

The LIMBOURG brothers

6

7

8

9

10

Les Très Riches Heures du duc de Berry 1415

1

2

3

4

5

6

Jan VAN EYCK   Madonna

7

8

9

10

11

12

with Canon Van der Paele 1436

1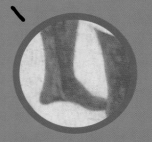

2

3

4

5

Paolo UCCELLO

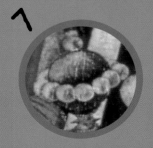

6 7 8 9 10

The Battle of San Romano   circa 1456

1

2

3

4

5

6

Benozzo GOZZOLI

16

7

8

9

10

11

The Procession of the Magi

1459

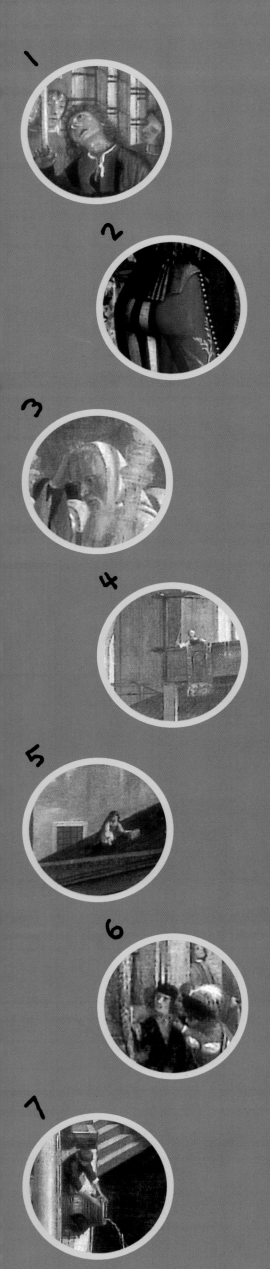

8

9

10

11

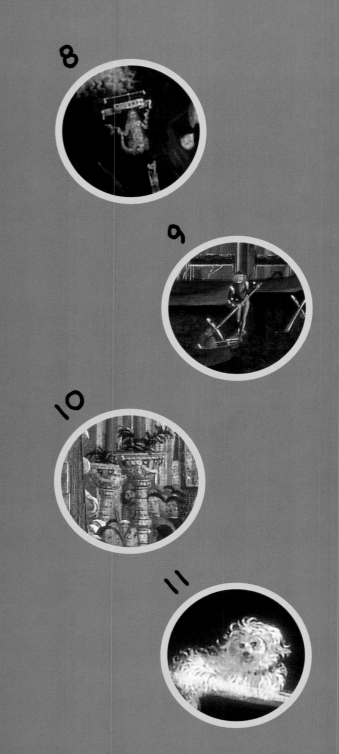

Vittore CARPACCIO

The Miracle of the Relic of the Holy Cross

circa 1500

1

2

3

4

5

Hieronymus BOSCH

6

7

8

9

10

The Temptation of Saint Anthony   circa **1500**

Aztec manuscript Codex Borbonicus

early **16**th **century**

early 16th century

23

1

2

3

4

5

Les Vendanges tapestry

6

7

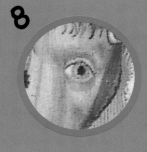
8

9

10

early **16**th **century**

25

Pieter BRUEGEL the Elder

The Battle between Carnival and Lent
1559

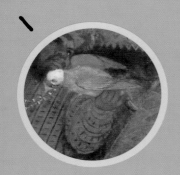

1

2

3

4

5

6

Paolo VERONESE

28

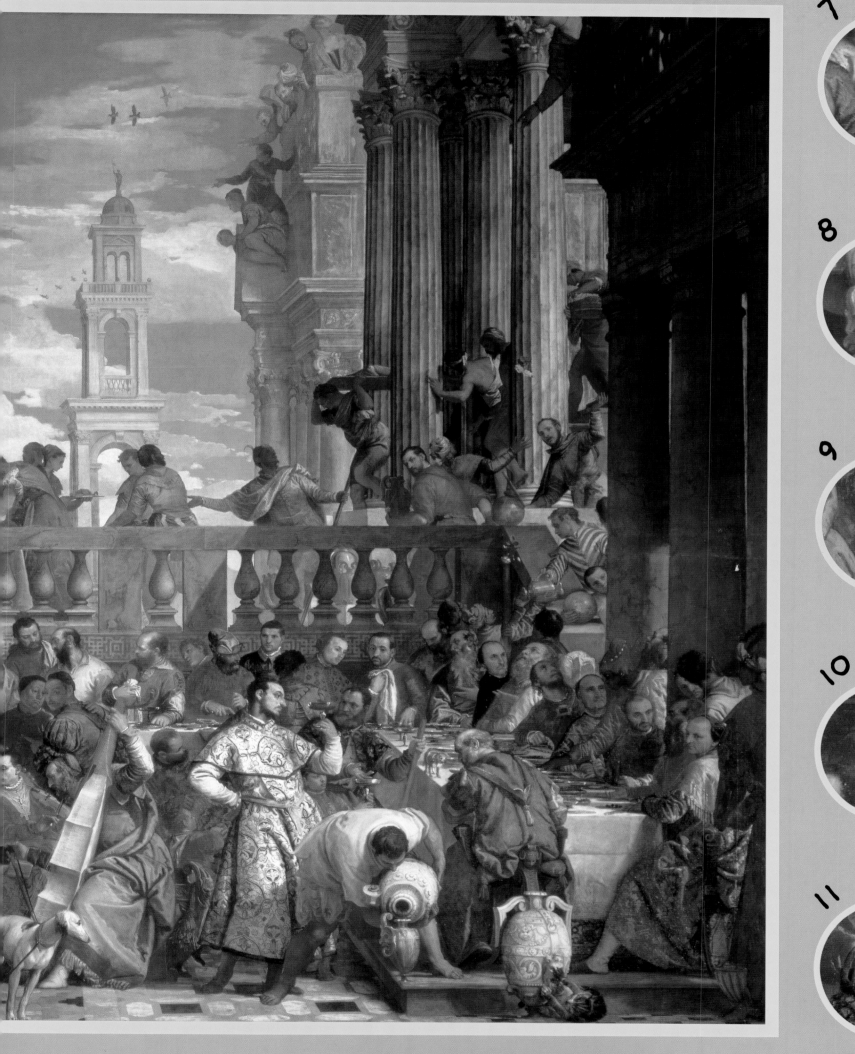

7

8

9

10

11

The Marriage at Cana

1562

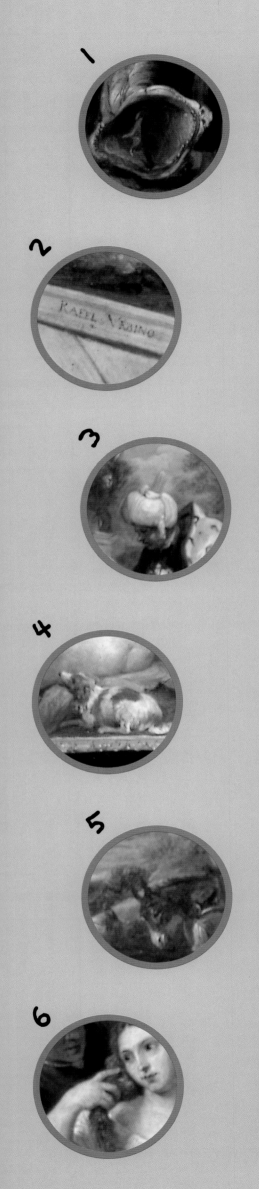

1

2

3

4

5

6

David TENIERS the Younger

Archduke Leopold-William in
His Gallery in Brussels

31

1651

Jan STEEN

The Village School

1665

33

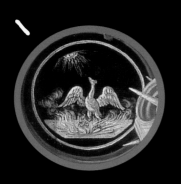

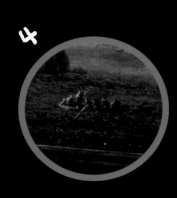

Domenico REMPS Cabinet of

34

6

7

8

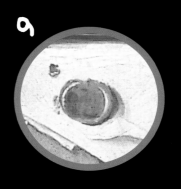
9

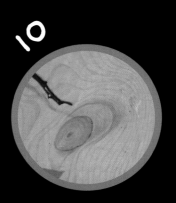
10

Curiosities   late 17th century

35

1

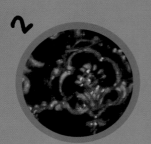
2

3

4

5

Antoine WATTEAU

36

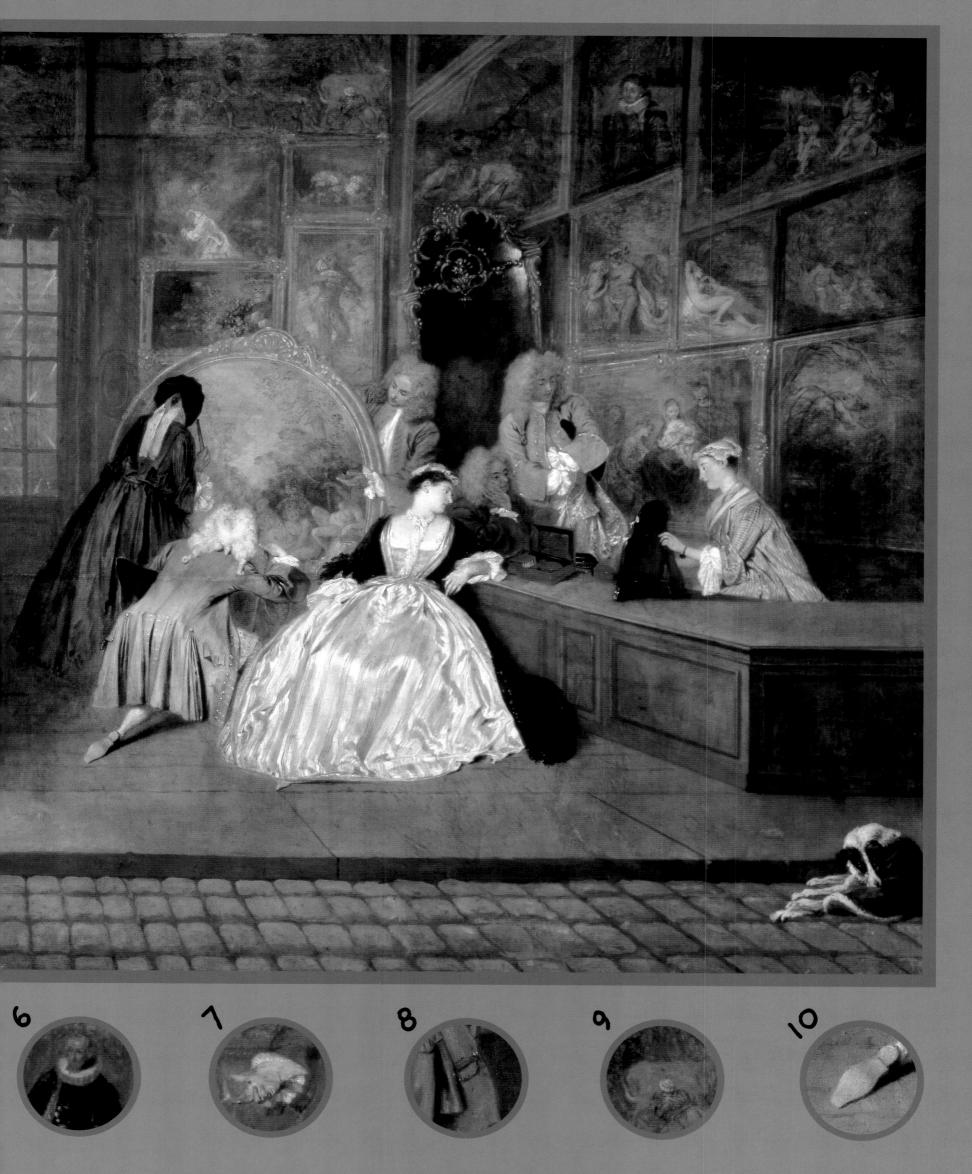

6 7 8 9 10

L'Enseigne de Gersaint   1720

1

2

3

4

5

Utagawa KUNISADA

38

6

7

8

9

10

The Oath of Loyalty
in the Peach Garden

early 19th century

39

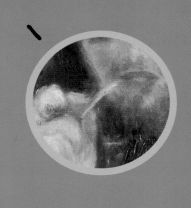

1

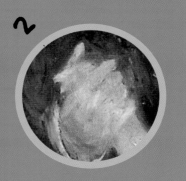

3

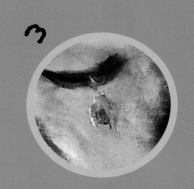

4

5

6

Pierre Auguste RENOIR

40

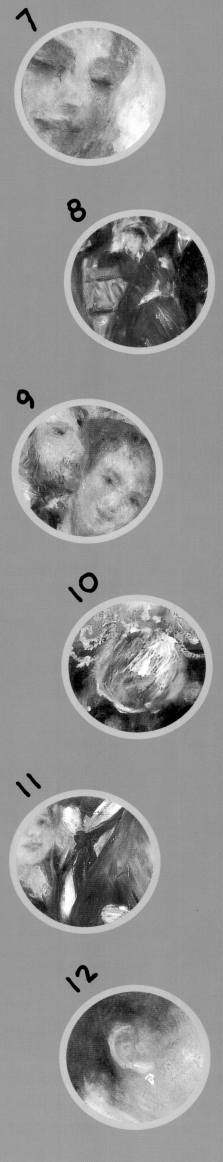

Le Moulin de la Galette

1876

FANFARES
DOCTRINAIRES
TOUJOURS
REUSSI

1

2

3

4

ENSOR
1888

5

James ENSOR

Christ's

6

7

8

9

10

Entry into Brussels

1888

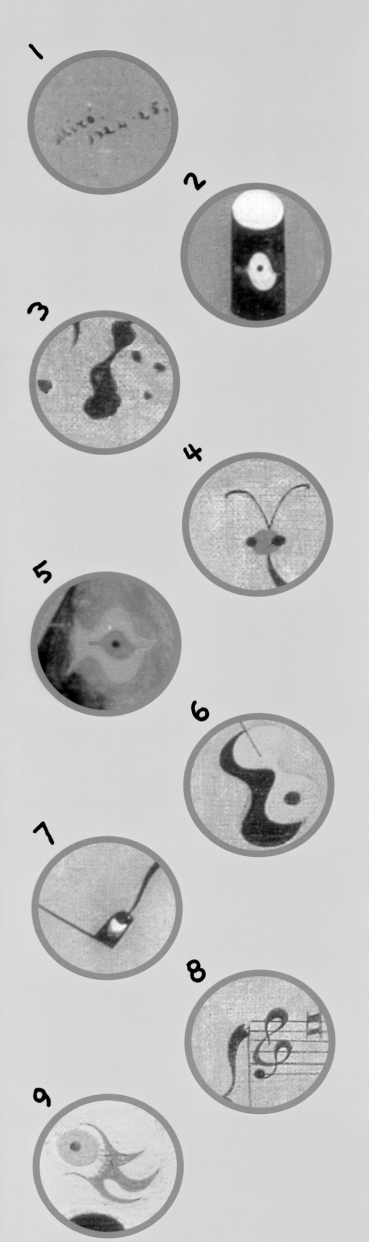

1

2

3

4

5

6

7

8

9

Joan MIRÓ

The Harlequin's Carnival 1924

1
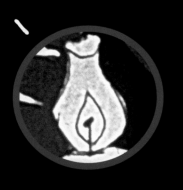

2

3
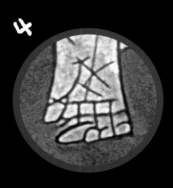

4

5

Pablo PICASSO

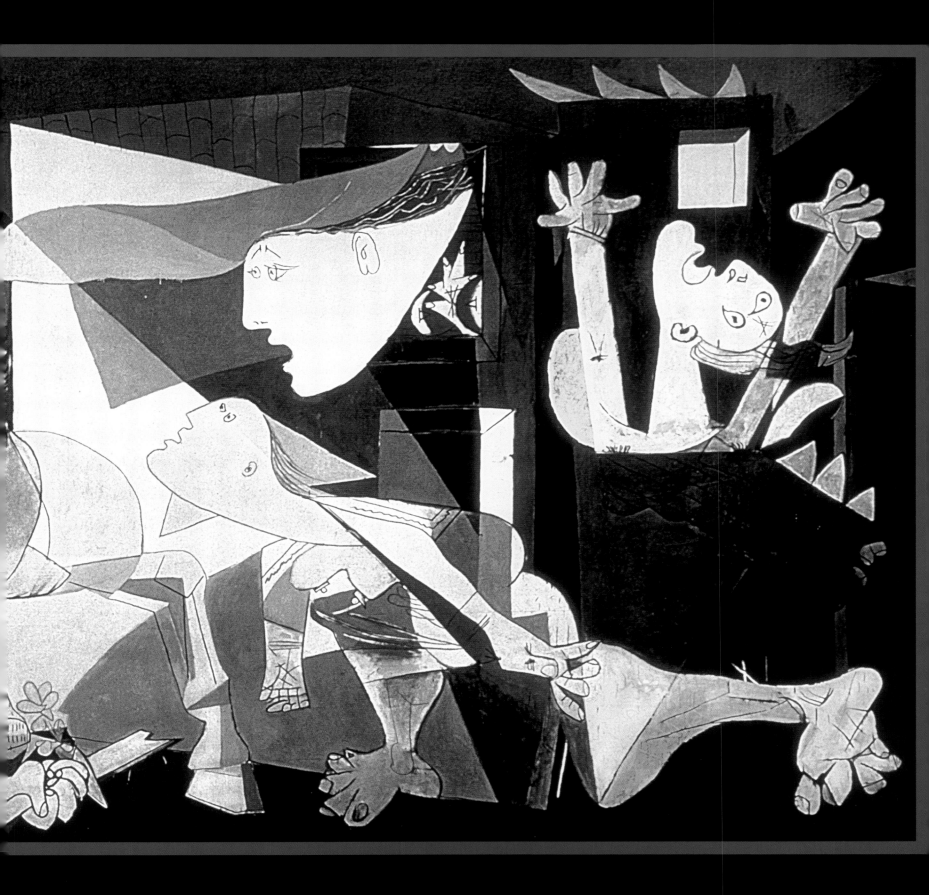

6

7

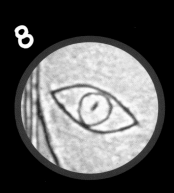

8

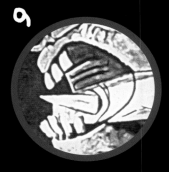

9

10

Guernica

1937

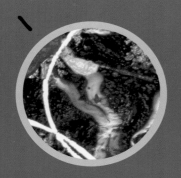

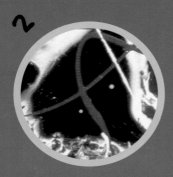

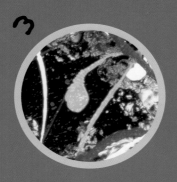

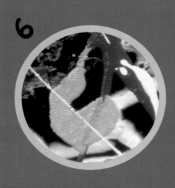

1

2

3

4

5

6

Jackson POLLOCK

48

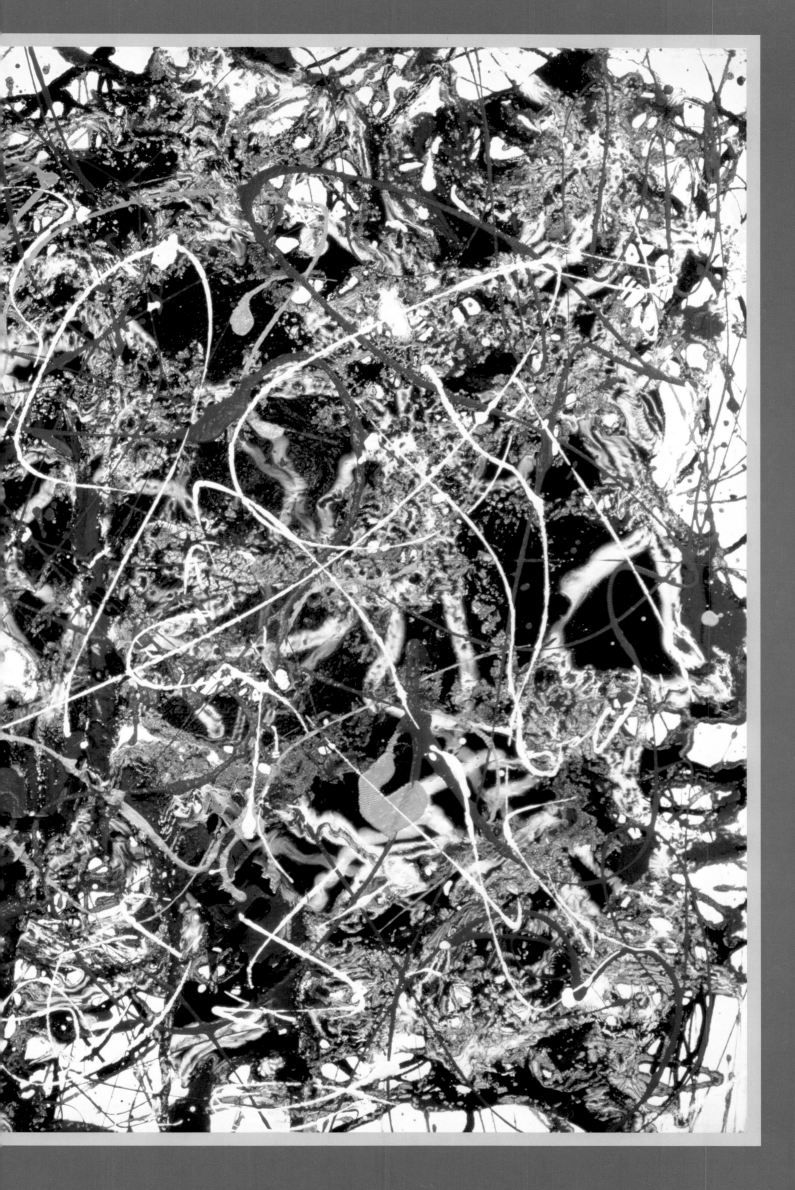

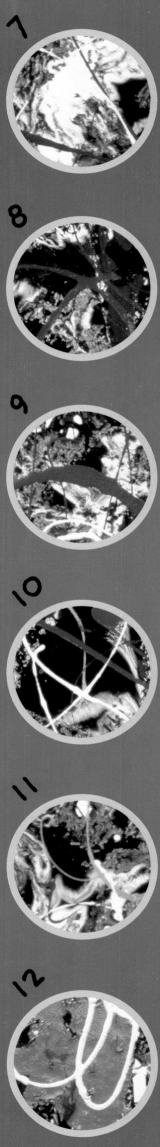

7

8

9

10

11

12

Number 6

1948

49

AT THE HEART OF THE PYRAMIDS: The Egyptian Books of the Dead

Five thousand years ago, on the banks of the Nile River, one of the oldest civilizations was born. For the pharaohs, or kings, of ancient Egypt, death was the entrance to eternity. But in order to gain eternal life, certain rites had to be performed. When a pharaoh or a nobleman died, his body was embalmed, mummified, and buried with special objects. The walls of his tomb and the lining of his sarcophagus were decorated with scenes from his life. A scroll containing instructions for his future life was placed near his body. This type of scroll was called a "book of the dead." It was made from the fibers of the papyrus plant that grew along the banks of the Nile. The scrolls were several yards long and were carefully illustrated by scribes who knew how to write using signs called "hieroglyphs." When the scribes drew humans and gods, they drew their heads, arms, and legs in profile and their eyes, shoulders, and chests from the front. The artists weren't trying to make their drawings look realistic; instead, they wanted to show their subjects' most important features as clearly as possible. **(Page 4)**

THE GOLD OF BYZANTIUM: Pictures in a Thousand Pieces

In the fourth century, the emperor of Rome converted to Christianity. The ancient city of Byzantium was renamed Constantinople and became the eastern capital of his empire. The style of the churches built around this time came to be called Byzantine. Byzantine churches of the sixth century looked somber on the outside but were richly decorated inside. To symbolize the power and eternity of God—as well as that of the emperor, who was believed to be God's agent on earth—the walls were covered with mosaics. Artists created mosaics like *The Sacrifice of Isaac* using cubes of glass for red, yellow, and green. For white, black, and brown, they used pieces of marble or mother-of-pearl. These tiny pieces of glass and stone reflected light in a way that dazzled those who looked at them and reminded them of the divine light. Byzantine artworks like this one inspired the medieval artists of Western Europe. **(Page 6)**

PAPER AND CALLIGRAPHY: Islamic Manuscripts

In the seventh century, not long after the death of Mohammed, the founder of Islam, Arab culture began to spread across the globe. In the ninth century, Arabs began using paper, a Chinese invention, to make books. To copy the Koran, the sacred book that recounts the teachings of Mohammed, Arab artists perfected the art of handwriting, or calligraphy. Books quickly multiplied—not only religious works, but scholarly essays on medicine, astronomy, and astrology, such as *The Book of Nativities* by Abu Ma'shar. The pages of this book are filled with horoscopes, which predict the future through the positions of the planets on the day a person was born. The faces of the sun and moon are each circled by a disk, and the planets are represented as human figures. For example, Venus plays a musical instrument and Saturn waves an axe. **(Page 8)**

PAINTED BOOKS: The Art of Illumination

In monasteries across Europe during the Middle Ages, monks copied the Bible onto sheets of parchment that they decorated with paintings called "illuminations." From the thirteenth century on, artists working for powerful lords also created illuminated manuscripts. Every great royal figure possessed a book of hours— a book of prayers to recite at different times of the day. The Limbourg brothers created one for the duke Jean de Berry. Like other books of its kind, the Duc de Berry's book of hours began with an illustrated calendar. The page illustrating January shows the duke, seated in his splendid blue robe, receiving his admirers. The page illustrating August shows elegantly dressed couples leaving for a falcon hunt, while crops are being harvested outside the castle walls. These illustrations showed the splendor and luxury of life in the duke's court. To create the many fine details in these scenes, the three Limbourg brothers almost certainly used a magnifying glass and extremely slender paintbrushes. **(Page 10)**

THE SECRET OF VAN EYCK: The Revolution of Oil Painting

Flemish painter Jan Van Eyck worked by painting thin layers of color, first opaque then translucent, on wooden panels. The light that shines through his paintings comes from a special concoction that he developed. At the time, painters couldn't go to the store and buy paints as they can today. Instead, their apprentices ground clay and other substances to create colored powders called "pigments." Most artists then mixed these pigments with egg white to form a paste that was hard to paint with because it dried very quickly. But Van Eyck revived an ancient technique: He mixed his pigments with oil. Oil paint dried very slowly, so Van Eyck had time to add precise touches and blend colors. As a result his paintings look more realistic. Rich and powerful patrons often commissioned religious works from artists, who often included images of their patrons in the paintings. Van Eyck painted the man who commissioned *Madonna with Canon Van der Paele* kneeling next to the Virgin Mary. **(Page 12)**

THE INVENTION OF PERSPECTIVE: The Renaissance

Like many other artists of the fifteenth century, Paolo Uccelo was extremely interested in making his paintings look three-dimensional. The fifteenth century was a time when great navigators were exploring the globe and people were rediscovering ancient ideas through books made available by the newly invented printing press. These changes created a revolution in thought and lifestyle that we call the Renaissance. Sculptors, architects, and painters began to look for ways to represent the world scientifically. To do this they developed a technique called "perspective," which allows far-away objects to appear smaller than nearby objects, the way they do in real life. In 1456, Paolo Uccello painted *The Battle of San Romano* on three wooden panels for the palace of the Medici, one of the most powerful families in Florence. In this depiction of the victory of Florence over the nearby city of Sienna, he created distance and space by means of geometric shapes. Uccello structured the painting as a series of lines moving back toward the horizon. Even the lines of the weapons in the air and on the ground add to the effect. **(Page 14)**

PAINTING ON THE WALLS: The Art of Fresco

During the same period that Uccello was mastering perspective, the Medici family commissioned Benozzo Gozzoli to decorate the walls of the chapel in its palace in Florence. He painted the journey of the Magi, the three wise men who visited the baby Jesus, as they traveled to Bethlehem. Nearly one hundred lords, pages, and soldiers follow the Magi, displaying Gozzoli's skill for portrait. One of these figures bears the features of Lorenzo de' Medici. To create this fresco, Gozzoli first drew the scene on paper, then poked tiny holes along the outlines of all the shapes in it. Next, he held the paper to the wall and stamped it with a canvas bag of ochre or charcoal, which penetrated the holes and transferred the outlines of his drawing onto the wall. Gozzoli then coated a section of the wall with a layer of plaster—sand and fresh lime—and while it was still wet, applied his colors, each made from earth diluted with water. He divided the surface of the wall into "days"—sections that he could finish in a single day, each nine or ten square feet. He had to work quickly before the plaster dried and "imprisoned" the painting on the wall. Although frescoes existed in ancient times, it wasn't until the fourteenth century that the great Italian master Giotto perfected the technique. Frescoes decorated many monuments built in Italy during this time. **(Page 16)**

A NEW SUPPORT: Canvas

Artists started painting on canvas stretched over frames in the middle of the fifteenth century. Made from hemp, linen, or even nettles, canvas was much cheaper and lighter than wood and could be rolled up or folded in order to be transported. It was particularly appreciated in Venice, a humid city where frescoes did not keep well and wood was rare. Like many Venetian painters, Vittore Carpaccio painted many of his works on canvas. He used historical and religious themes to show life in Venice in the fifteenth century, then one of the richest cities in Europe. In his painting *Miracle of the Relic of the Holy Cross,* he illustrates the healing of a man possessed by the devil. **(Page 18)**

A PUZZLE TEEMING WITH DEVILS: The Medieval Universe of Bosch

Flemish painter Hieronymus Bosch peopled his paintings with eerie forms and strange monsters that made his works very different from the Italian painters of the Renaissance. In his triptych (a painting on three connected panels) called *The Temptation of Saint Anthony,* his fantastic creatures combine features of objects, animals, and people. Each of his bizarre details has a symbolic significance that is often difficult to understand today. Saint Anthony was a hermit who went into the desert to pray and had to resist the devils that tried to tempt him while he was there. The struggle between the forces of good and evil was an idea that especially interested people at the end of the Middle Ages, when almost everyone believed in the existence of God, the devil, and hell. Bosch, who lived near the end of the Middle Ages, used the new artistic discoveries of the Renaissance, such as perspective, to create paintings that still reflected a medieval view of the world. **(Page 20)**

SCREENFOLDS: The Aztec Codexes

The Renaissance was an era of great exploration in which Europeans "discovered" the rest of the world. In 1519, the Spanish conquered what is now Mexico, ruled at the time by the Aztecs. The Spanish conquistadores encountered a civilization that until then had been entirely unknown to Europeans. The Aztecs believed in many gods who made terrifying demands. They required continual offerings of human hearts to keep the world turning. Knowledge of astronomy and science allowed the Aztecs to fix the dates of the sacred ceremonies in which they performed their human sacrifices. The *Codex Borbonicus,* completed around 1500, is a calendar that was used by the astronomer-priests.

To create this codex, the Aztecs made a long sheet of paper using fibers from the agave plant, then folded it like an accordion. Painted in vivid colors, this strange "comic strip" features figures that were either real or symbolic. **(Page 22)**

WOVEN "PAINTINGS": Tapestries

During the fourteenth and fifteenth centuries, tapestries played an important role in the lives of the nobility and wealthy merchants. Hung on the cold, damp stone walls of castles, tapestries helped keep the rooms warm and protected against drafts. They also made rooms cozier by enlivening them with their colorful pictures. Tapestries are woven in wool and sometimes highlighted with silk or even gold or silver thread. Weavers created these fabric paintings on looms, strand by strand, copying drawings called "cartoons." Tapestries often represent religious or historical scenes. But sometimes they represent scenes of everyday life, as does the *Les Vendanges* (French for "Wine Making") tapestry. Nearly fifteen feet long, it shows men and women cutting grapes, heaping them into baskets, and transporting them to large vats to be crushed. A lord and a lady, dressed in elegant clothes, pass by and taste the grapes. Are they the ones who commissioned this tapestry? **(Page 24)**

THE REPRESENTATION OF EVERYDAY LIFE: Genre Painting

In the sixteenth century, art changed in a radical way when Protestants in northern Europe began to oppose what they saw as the Catholic church's cult of sacred images. As a result, many artists in Protestant areas turned to nonreligious themes, such as scenes of everyday life. This was the birth of what we call "genre painting." Pieter Bruegel the Elder painted with realism and humor the joys and miseries of peasants as they labored and feasted. Looking closely at the crowds that fill his paintings, you can see that Bruegel paid attention to every detail of their clothing, tools, and belongings. *The Battle of Carnival and Lent* is an imaginary scene showing the meeting between fat Carnival (the huge celebration held just before Lent), who holds in his hand a pig on a spit, and skinny Lent (the forty days before Easter, which people usually spent fasting and praying), who is brandishing a couple of fish. Nothing in the painting appears by accident—even the tiny eggshells on the ground indicate that carnival waffles are being prepared nearby. **(Page 26)**

A SYMPHONY OF COLORS: Venetian Artists

Painters in sixteenth-century Italy frequently belonged to the guild, or association, of color merchants. They began as apprentices, performing small tasks in their masters' workshops, such as sweeping the studio or grinding colored pigments. If they were skillful, their masters would eventually give them more difficult jobs, such as preparing the painting surfaces or sketching out and coloring a small section of a painting. At the end of six or eight years of apprenticeship, they became journeymen; after several more years they could earn the title "master." When he was about twenty-five, Paolo Veronese became a master and opened his own workshop in Venice. He created *Marriage at Cana* to decorate the dining hall of a convent. The painting is more than nine feet long and shows Christ's first miracle, the transformation of water into wine. It reveals much about the life of sixteenth-century nobles, who are shown dressed in expensive clothes and surrounded by luxury. Veronese was more interested in the beauty and harmony of the colors used than he was with what he painted. **(Page 28)**

OBJECTS TO COLLECT: Paintings

As the art trade grew in the seventeenth century, so did the number of art collectors. Collectors preferred smaller paintings, which were easier to transport and display. Kings, princes, and rich bankers installed their collections in large galleries. The religious images, portraits, and mythological scenes that covered the walls of these galleries displayed the wealth and good taste of their owner. In 1651, David Teniers the Younger painted the archduke Leopold-William, governor of the Spanish Netherlands, in his gallery full of works by well-known artists such as Rubens and Raphael. Eventually, the public was allowed in to see many of these collections, and the great European museums were born. **(Page 30)**

LIGHT AND CHIAROSCURO: Dutch Painting

In the seventeenth century, members of the Dutch middle class bought paintings of still lifes, landscapes, portraits, and interior scenes to decorate the walls of their houses. Painter Jan Steen was talented at recreating scenes of everyday life. His paintings, set in taverns, feasts, and baptisms, gave the impression of life unfolding before the viewer's eyes. Looking at his painting *The Village School*, we have the feeling of being in a classroom. While the schoolmaster studies his quills, the children are left alone to talk with each other, play games, and make a mess. Steen used light to highlight their faces and bring them out of the shadows that fill the rest of the picture. Rembrandt, the greatest Dutch artist of the seventeenth century, was the first Northern painter to master this effect, called "chiaroscuro" (pronounced *kyar-ah-SKOO-ro*). **(Page 32)**

THE ART OF ILLUSION: Still Life and Trompe l'Oeil

Until the end of the Renaissance, objects were featured only as details in paintings. But from the beginning of the seventeenth century on, especially in Northern Europe, objects became the main subjects of paintings called "still lifes." Sometimes the artists were so successful at creating the illusion of reality that the objects in the paintings seemed real, a technique called "trompe l'oeil" (pronounced *trump loy*) which means "trick the eye" in French. *In The Cabinet of Curiosities,* Domenico Remps, master of trompe l'oeil, makes an entire armoire containing a collection of objects appear unbelievably real. Armoires like the one he painted were known as "cabinets of curiosities." In them princes would collect paintings, sculptures, and the scientific, zoological, and botanical discoveries that excited so much curiosity at the time. Often in paintings of these cabinets, an object such as a clock or a skull appears. It symbolizes death or the passing of time, making viewers put in perspective the value of these "curiosities" and the vanity of their collectors. **(Page 34)**

A MELANCHOLY POETRY: Eighteenth—Century French Painting

Antoine Watteau filled his notebooks with rapidly drawn, precise sketches. His drawings could capture the expression of a face, an attitude, or a spontaneous gesture. He then would compose a painting by putting together these small sketches from his notebooks. Watteau often painted *fêtes galantes*—the elegant outdoor parties that were fashionable in the eighteenth century. His paintings mark a turning point in the history of art. They are intended to communicate the state of the artist's soul; their subjects are less important. Watteau sought to make paintings that, like music, would create an emotion in the viewer. Not long before his death, he spent a couple of days painting this sign for the new shop of his friend, the art dealer Gersaint. It was a very unusual thing for a painter of his rank to do. The two panels show Gersaint's shop. The canvases on the walls and the gestures of the people in the shop all help to make the viewer feel like a part of the murmur of conversation among the clients and the salespeople. The portrait being lowered into a crate is of King Louis XIV of France, who died five years before. **(Page 36)**

WOOD CARVING IN COLOR: The Japanese Woodblock Print

To create a woodblock print, an ink drawing on paper was glued onto a block of peach or cherry wood. The artist then carved the surface of the wood, leaving the outlines of shapes and certain areas of the drawing raised ("in relief"). Next, the block was covered with ink and pressed onto paper like a stamp. To create multicolored prints, a different block of wood had to be carved for each color used. In Japan only nobles were allowed to have paintings, so woodblock prints became very popular among the urban middle class in the eighteenth and nineteenth centuries. Known as *ukiyo-e* (pronounced *oo-kee-yo-AY*), the prints often showed landscapes, scenes of everyday life, or the theater. In this print Utagawa Kunisada illustrates a common theme in Japanese art: an oath of loyalty taken by three heroes before they depart on a conquest of foreign lands. In 1854, when Japanese ports opened to foreign traders, woodblock prints found their way to America and Europe, where they fascinated and inspired the Impressionists. **(Page 38)**

PAINTING OUTDOORS: Impressionism

In 1874, a show of paintings in Paris created a scandal. The critics mocked the exhibited works, especially Claude Monet's *Impression: Sunrise*. In reference to the painters' "hurried" style, the critics called the painters "Impressionists." But these Impressionists had started a revolution. Until then, since painters had to mix their paints themselves they mostly painted scenes they created in their studios and carefully planned out their works. But the invention of paint in tubes made it easy for artists to carry painting supplies out of the studio, which allowed the Impressionists to set up their easels outdoors. There they sought to capture the quickly changing light and the fleeting impressions of a moment. They used the pure colors that came from the tubes to show light vibrating across the canvas. Only two years after the first Impressionist show in 1876, Pierre Auguste Renoir painted *Le Moulin de la Galette,* which is the name of the Parisian dance hall in the painting. Renoir loved to capture the atmosphere and look of people in real places. Sunlight dances on the dancers' dresses and faces, and Renoir's loose brushstrokes make their outlines seem to blur. **(Page 40)**

COLORS THAT CRY OUT: Toward Expressionism

From the window of his studio, James Ensor observed the people who filled the streets of Ostend, a fashionable seaside resort in the north of Belgium. These crowds inhabit his works, in particular an immense painting called *Christ's Entry into Brussels,* which blends reality and fantasy. Ensor uses gaudy colors to paint a dense crowd that appears to spill out of the borders of the painting. Figures wear death and clown masks and military and clerical uniforms. These grotesque characters, confused or sneering and not at all lifelike, demonstrate Ensor's feelings about his fellow humans. We can almost hear the brouhaha of the blues, reds, and greens in the painting. The paint is built up on the canvas, kneaded, and scratched. Ensor was the first painter in a movement that came to be called "Expressionism." At the beginning of the twentieth century, particularly in Germany, the Expressionists "expressed" their stormy, changing feelings by using violent colors and painting aggressive subjects. These painters tried to show sensations and emotions more than external reality. **(Page 42)**

THE PAINTING OF DREAMS: Surrealism

After the First World War, writers, painters, and sculptors looked for new ways to express themselves that broke with tradition. They wanted to bring together dream and reality and logic and nonsense in a sort of total reality—"surreality." Miró was one of the great Surrealist painters, and his *The Harlequin's Carnival* is the most characteristic painting of this movement. In it, little fantastical creatures, which aren't much more than shapes, celebrate a carnival. A harlequin (clown) with a red-and-blue face smokes a pipe, a mechanical guitarist makes music, and two cats play. The painting is filled with strange objects found in other Miró works: ladders, flames, stars, eyes, fish, circles, cones, discs, and lines. In Miró's poetic and fantastic universe, each of these forms, lines, and colors is symbolic of an emotion or a concept. As he wrote, he wished his work to be "like a poem put to music by a painter." **(Page 44)**

At the start of the twentieth century, two painters, Georges Braque and Pablo Picasso, invented a revolutionary style of painting called Cubism. In his Cubist paintings, Picasso draws objects and people from many different angles—at the same time—as if he were turning around them and showing several different sides at once. He constructed his paintings like an architect and arranged all the shapes geometrically, almost like blueprints. Picasso was trying to show the structure of things rather than how they looked. In 1937, Picasso painted *Guernica,* a giant work showing the mass murder of women and children in Guernica, Spain, during the Spanish Civil War. This painting is like a cry of despair at the cruelty of man. Open mouths with dagger-shaped tongues, bleeding hands, desperate expressions, and bodies in painful-looking poses all express fear and suffering. *Guernica* is painted in black, gray, and white, the colors of mourning and of the newspapers that reported these tragic events. It is one of the major works of one of the most famous artists of the twentieth century. **(Page 46)**

FREE AND PERSONAL PAINTINGS: Abstract Expressionism

"I continue to get further away from the usual painter's tools such as the easel, palette, brushes, etc. I prefer sticks, trowels, knives, and dripping fluid paint. . . ." From 1947 on, the American artist Jackson Pollock began to paint on huge canvases that he spread on the floor so that he could be directly "in" his paintings. As he circled *Number 6,* he poured and flung paint over the surface of the canvas to create a tangle of lines. Pollock made thick splashes and puddles of blue paint, then cast yellow and red spots on top of them. He painted violently and freely, letting the rhythm of his gestures direct how he put paint onto the canvas. What he painted were not pictures of things or people but his own movements, which is why his work has been called "action painting." Pollock paved the way to a new artistic movement called "Abstract Expressionism" that spread across the United States and then Europe in the 1950s. **(Page 48)**

Egyptian papyrus
From **The Book of the Dead**
by the royal scribe Hu-Nefer
circa 1300 B.C.

Arabic manuscript
The Book of Nativities by Abu Ma'shar
15ᵗʰ century A.D.

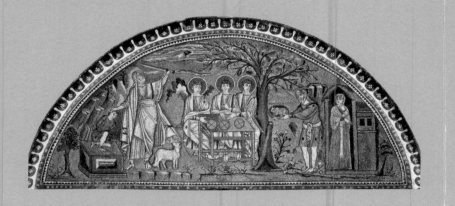

Byzantine mosaic
The Sacrifice of Isaac
6ᵗʰ century A.D.

The LIMBOURG brothers
Les Très Riches Heures du Duc de Berry
1415

Jan VAN EYCK
Madonna with Canon Van der Paele
1436

Paolo UCCELLO
The Battle of San Romano
circa 1456

Benozzo GOZZOLI
The Procession of the Magi
1459

Vittore
CARPACCIO
**The Miracle of
the Relic of the
Holy Cross**
circa 1500

Hieronymus BOSCH
The Temptation of Saint Anthony
circa 1500

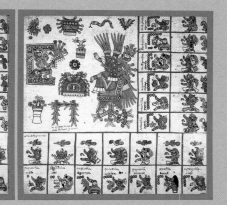

Aztec manuscript
Codex Borbonicus
early 16th century

Les Vendanges tapestry
early 16th century

Paolo VERONESE
The Marriage at Cana
1562

David TENIERS the Younger
**Archduke Leopold—William
in His Gallery in Brussels**
1651

Jan STEEN
The Village School
1665

Domenico REMPS
Cabinet of Curiosities
late 17th century

Antoine WATTEAU
L'Enseigne de Gersaint
1720

62

Utagawa KUNISADA
The Oath of Loyalty in the Peach Garden
early 19ᵗʰ century

Pierre Auguste RENOIR
Le Moulin de la Galette
1876

James ENSOR
Christ's Entry into Brussels
1888

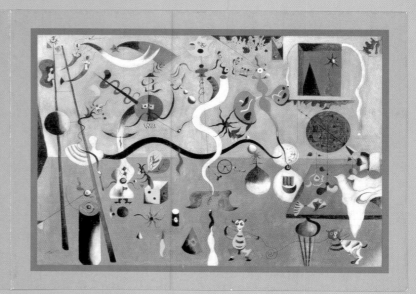

Joan MIRÓ
The Harlequin's Carnival
1924

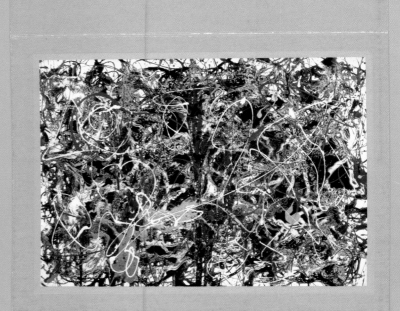

Pablo PICASSO
Guernica
1937

Jackson POLLOCK
Number 6
1948

WHERE ARE THE WORKS OF ART IN THIS BOOK EXHIBITED?

- pp. 4 and 5 and jacket: British Museum, London (United Kingdom)

- pp. 6 and 7: Church of San Vitale, Ravenna (Italy)

- pp. 8 and 9: Bibliothèque Nationale de France, Paris (France)

- pp. 10 and 11 and cover: Musée Condé, Chantilly (France)

- pp. 12 and 13: Groeningemuseum, Bruges (Belgium)

- pp. 14 and 15: National Gallery, London (United Kingdom)

- pp. 16 and 17: Palazzo Medici-Riccardi, Florence (Italy)

- pp. 18 and 19: Galleria dell'Accademia, Venice (Italy)

- pp. 20 and 21: Museu Nacional de Arte Antiga, Lisbon (Portugal)

- pp. 22 and 23: Bibliothèque de l'Assemblée Nationale, Paris (France)

- pp. 24 and 25: Musée National des Thermes et de l'Hôtel de Cluny, Paris (France)

- pp. 26 and 27 and title page: Kunsthistorisches Museum, Vienna (Austria)

- pp. 28 and 29: Musée du Louvre, Paris (France)

- pp. 30 and 31: Museo del Prado, Madrid (Spain)

- pp. 32 and 33: National Gallery of Scotland, Edinburgh (United Kingdom)

- pp. 34 and 35: Opificio delle Pietre Dure, Florence (Italy)

- pp. 36 and 37: Schloss Charlottenburg, Berlin (Germany)

- pp. 38 and 39: Private collection

- pp. 40 and 41: Musée d'Orsay, Paris (France)

- pp. 42 and 43: The J. Paul Getty Museum, Los Angeles (United States)

- pp. 44 and 45: Albright-Knox Art Gallery, Buffalo, New York (United States)

- pp. 46 and 47: Museo Nacional Centro de Arte Reina Sofia, Madrid (Spain)

- pp. 48 and 49: James Goodman Gallery, New York City (United States)

PHOTOGRAPHIC CREDITS